D0108430

Spring

by Gail Saunders-Smith

Content Consultant:
Lisa M. Nyberg, Ph.D.
Educator, Springfield (Oregon) Public Schools

an imprint of Capstone Press

Pebble Books

Pebble Books are published by Capstone Press
818 North Willow Street, Mankato, Minnesota 56001
http://www.capstone-press.com

Library of Congress Cataloging-in-Publication Data
Saunders-Smith, Gail.
    Spring/by Gail Saunders-Smith.
        p. cm.
    Includes bibliographical references and index.
    Summary: Simple text and photographs depict the weather, plants, animals, and activities
of spring.
    ISBN 1-56065-781-2
    1. Spring—Juvenile literature. [1. Spring.] I. Title.
    QB637.5.S28 1998
    508.2—dc21   98-5050
                                                              CIP
                                                              AC

Note to Parents and Teachers

This book describes and illustrates the changes in weather, people, plants, and animals in spring. The close picture-text matches support early readers in understanding the text. The text offers subtle challenges with compound and complex sentence structures. This book also introduces early readers to expository and content-specific vocabulary. The expository vocabulary is defined in the Words to Know section. Early readers may need assistance in reading some of these words. Readers also may need assistance in using the Table of Contents, Words to Know, Read More, Internet Sites, and Index/Word List sections of the book.

Table of Contents

4

Spring is a season for beginning. Spring comes after winter and before summer.

The snow begins to melt. The days begin to warm. The sun shines, and the rain falls.

People put away their winter clothes. They play outside. They ride bikes and fly kites.

People work outside, too.
Farmers plant seeds in fields.
People plant seeds in gardens.

Seeds begin to grow. Stems appear above the soil. Plants grow. Flowers bloom.

Leaves grow on trees and bushes. Grass turns from brown to green.

16

Some bears, bats, and snakes hibernate in winter. Hibernate is to sleep deeply. These animals wake up in spring. They look for food.

18

Many birds fly north in spring.
They build nests and lay eggs.
Chicks hatch from the eggs.

Deer, rabbits, and foxes give birth to young. Frog eggs become tadpoles. Spring is a season for beginning.

Words to Know

bud—the part of a plant that grows into a flower or leaf

field—a piece of land where farmers grow plants

hatch—to come out of an egg

hibernate—to sleep deeply through winter

melt—to soften and become like water

plow—to break up the ground and prepare it for planting

season—one of the four parts of a year; spring, summer, autumn, and winter

sprout—to start to grow into a plant; the first part of a plant to come out of the ground

stem—the long part of a plant that carries water and food between the leaves and the roots

tadpole—a young frog; a tadpole has a tail and lives in the water

Read More

Gibbons, Gail. *The Reasons for Seasons.* New York: Holiday House, 1995.

Muller, Gerda. *Circle of Seasons.* New York: Dutton Children's Books, 1995.

Schweninger, Ann. *Springtime.* Let's Look at the Seasons. New York: Viking, 1993.

 # Internet Sites

4 Seasons: Spring
http://www.rescol.ca/collections/agriculture/qfa4sea.html

INTELLICast: Spring Is the Severe Weather Season
http://www.intellicast.com/drdew/archive/svrwx.html

Signs of the Seasons
http://www.4seasons.org.uk/projects/seasons/index.html

Index/Word List

Word Count: 142
Early-Intervention Level: 9

Editorial Credits

Lois Wallentine, editor; Timothy Halldin, design; Michelle L. Norstad, photo research

Photo Credits

Betty Crowell, 14
Cheryl A. Ertlet, 16
International Stock/Dario Perla, 6; Bill Tucker, 8
KAC Productions/Kathy Adams Clark, 10
Dwight Kuhn, 1
Photo Network, Inc./Esbin-Anderson, 12
Root Resources/Anthony Mercieca, 17; Alan G. Nelson, 20
James P. Rowan, 4
Unicorn Stock Photos/Joel Dexter, cover